DUTCH & FLEMISH PAINTING

Christopher Brown

TIGER BOOKS INTERNATIONAL
LONDON

The author and publishers are grateful to all museum
authorities and private owners who have given permission
for works in their possession to be reproduced. Plates 34,
49 and 54 are reproduced by gracious permission of
Her Majesty the Queen.

Original edition: Dutch & Flemish Painting
© 1977 by Phaidon Press Limited, Oxford
Reprinted 1985
© 1989 by Phaidon Press Limited, Oxford
For this special edition
© 1989 by I.P. Verlagsgesellschaft
International Publishing GmbH., München
Published in 1989 for
Tiger Books International PLC, London
ISBN 1-870461-71-1
Printed and bound by Brepols N.V., Turnhout, Belgium

Dutch and Flemish painting

In 1555 the Habsburg Emperor Charles V transferred the government of the Netherlands to his eldest son, Philip II, whom he also created King of Spain. At that time representatives of all the seventeen provinces of the Netherlands comprised the assembly of the States General at Brussels, and Charles and Philip appeared together before it on this occasion. During the course of Philip's reign, the whole of the Netherlands rose in revolt, but only the seven provinces to the north of the great rivers which flow into the North Sea succeeded in gaining their independence from Spanish rule. When the Twelve Years' Truce was signed in 1609 the division was clear: the north was to be independent and Protestant, the south remained subservient to Spain and reverted to Catholicism. This arrangement, largely the result of geographical and military factors, was formalized by the Treaty of Münster in 1648 (see Plate 47), and has survived (with a number of territorial changes) until the present day in the Netherlands and Belgium.

It is of major importance, therefore, when considering Dutch and Flemish art of the seventeenth century, to remember how recent the political split was, and that both schools of painting, however differently they developed, had common ancestry in the great school of early Netherlandish painting which flourished, principally in the towns of the south, in the fifteenth and sixteenth centuries. Rubens, for example, was born in 1577, only twenty-two years after Philip II's accession, at a time when the outcome of the revolt was very much in doubt.

Much of the fighting during the revolt took place in the south, and particularly in and around Antwerp. The resulting economic and social disruption, as well as the persecution of Protestants, caused many Flemings to seek refuge in the north. Among those emigrants were painters like Gillis van Coninxloo and David Vinckboons, who left Antwerp and finally settled in Amsterdam. Followers of Pieter Bruegel, they imported Flemish landscape and genre styles into Amsterdam, and influenced the younger generation of Dutch painters. For example, the great innovatory landscape artist Hercules Segers was a pupil of Coninxloo, and his more conservative contemporary Hendrick Avercamp (Plate 35) was probably a pupil of Vinckboons.

Both Dutch and Flemish seventeenth-century painting have their roots in early Netherlandish painting. However, it is undeniable that the two schools diverged markedly during the century, and there can be no doubt that this divergence in style and subject-matter was a direct result of the political and religious division between the two countries. In order to illustrate this divergence, the natural temptation is to compare the two leading figures of the century in the two countries: Rubens and Rembrandt. While such a comparison (which is attempted in this volume by a careful juxtaposition of plates) is immensely interesting and suggestive, it is not quite accurate. Rembrandt, one of the few Dutch painters who could equal Rubens in the range of his subject-matter (portraits, landscapes, reli-

gious and mythological subjects), is not representative of Dutch painters as a whole. Many Flemish painters, however, did emulate Rubens both in style and subject-matter (Van Dyck and Jordaens, for instance). Dutch artists tended to specialize in a way in which Flemish artists, on the whole, did not: Hals was exclusively a portraitist, de Hoogh a genre painter, Ruisdael a landscapist, and so on. They specialized in what they could do best, and what they knew would satisfy popular demand, and this question of demand, of patronage, is the crucial difference between the two countries.

In Flanders (the south), the traditional sources of patronage for artists remained predominant: the court, the aristocracy and the Catholic Church. Civic institutions and rich merchants also commissioned paintings, but there was no art market such as existed in Holland. This important difference can be best stated in this way: in Flanders, the great majority of paintings were individually commissioned (altarpieces, mythological and historical scenes, portraits, and so on), whereas in Holland the great majority of paintings were produced for the market. Holland had the first modern art market, which, with its apparatus of dealers, exhibitions and contracts, operated in a manner recognizably similar to the contemporary art market. This is not, of course, to say that no paintings were commissioned in Holland: nor, conversely, that a small art market did not exist in Flanders. Portraits are always commissioned by family or friends if not by the sitter himself, and it is no accident that such an enormous number of seventeenth-century Dutch portraits survive.

However, the traditional sources of patronage which dominated the production of paintings in Flanders in the seventeenth century no longer did so in Holland. The nearest equivalent to the court of the Archduke Albert and the Archduchess Isabella, the Regents of the King of Spain in Flanders, was the court of the Stadholder of Holland, the Prince of Orange, in The Hague. During the lifetime of Prince Frederik Henry and that of his consort Amalia van Solms, the House of Orange commissioned a considerable number of paintings and also painted decorations for the palaces at Rijswijk and Honselaersdijk (both now destroyed), and the Huis ten Bosch at The Hague. For the decoration of the latter (which still stands) with allegories of the House of Orange and the career of Frederik Henry, native artists like Gerard Honthorst and Cesar van Everdingen were employed, but imported Flemings, like Jacob Jordaens, played an important part. The style of these decorations was the international Baroque, a style suited to the glorification of princes, but out of place in the basically democratic Dutch Republic. It is significant that the series of religious paintings which Rembrandt executed for the Prince of Orange in the 1630s shows the artist at his most Baroque.

The financial resources of the House of Orange were small compared with the court at Brussels. Unlike the Flemish aristocracy, the Dutch nobles were few, politically impotent and relatively poor. They commissioned

portraits, but could not emulate their southern brethren in the elaborate decoration of their houses. Though there were more practising Catholics in the north (including a number of prominent painters, like Steen and Vermeer) than is generally appreciated, the Catholic Church had gone "underground" and could not commission altarpieces. The Calvinist churches, as can be seen in the church interiors of Saenredam (Plate 45), were white-washed and decorated only by hatchments.

Although these three traditional sources of patronage had been weakened or had disappeared altogether in the north, certain individuals and institutions did commission paintings other than single portraits. The new town hall in Amsterdam, for example, was decorated with scenes of the *Revolt of the Batavians* (seen as a prototype of the *Revolt of the Netherlands*) by leading Amsterdam painters, including Rembrandt. Other civic institutions commissioned paintings, as did the militia companies, directors of charitable foundations, and others. The group portrait of this kind is a uniquely Dutch phenomenon. But, despite these exceptions, most Dutch painters worked most of the time for the market. This had several important consequences. Firstly, paintings were cheap as there were so many of them. Holland in the seventeenth century was a rich country, benefiting from the success of her merchant navy, her merchants and her bankers, and yet this wealth, rather than being siphoned off by a few as happened elsewhere in Europe, does seem to have reached lower levels of society. It has been estimated that fifty per cent of the Dutch had some disposable income, that is to say, income over and above that devoted to necessities. Many ordinary Dutchmen, sailors and farmers, bought paintings, a fact which astonished visitors from England like John Evelyn.

The consequence of this popular demand was the production by a huge number of painters of an enormous number of paintings, which were bought and sold cheaply to decorate walls, rather than to be treasured as works of genius. This demand also affected the social status of the painter: rather than being a confidant of princes and nobles, as in the south, he was a craftsman, like a furniture maker or a potter, working for a popular market. A further consequence of this demand, was the emergence of many local schools of painting. Every town of any size had its own school: Delft, Dordrecht, Alkmaar, Hoorn, Deventer, Haarlem, and Leiden, for instance.

Holland is, therefore, the great exception in the history of seventeenth-century European painting. While certain stylistic similarities do exist, in terms of subject-matter and scale, Dutch painting differs greatly from the mainstream of the European Baroque, which found one of its greatest exponents in the Fleming, Rubens. Though geographically close neighbours, Dutch and Flemish seventeenth-century painters, both heirs to the same tradition, diverged radically during the course of the century as a direct result of the social, religious and political differences between their two countries.

The Captions

Peter Paul Rubens (1577–1640)
7   Study for the Figure of Christ on the Cross
Black and white chalk, some bistre wash, on coarse grey paper, $20\frac{3}{4} \times 14\frac{5}{8}$ in. About 1614–15. London, British Museum.

Hendrick Goltzius (1558–1616)
8   Quis Evadet Nemo (Who shall escape it?)
Pen, brown ink, $18\frac{1}{8} \times 14$ in. Signed with monogram and dated 1614. New York, Pierpont Morgan Library.

Jacob de Gheyn (1562–1629)
9   Allegory of Death
Pen, ink, grey and brown wash, $18 \times 13\frac{3}{4}$ in. Signed and dated 1599. London, British Museum.

Anthony Van Dyck (1599–1641)
10   A Man on Horseback and Three Horses' Heads
Brush and pen, with brown wash, $10\frac{3}{8} \times 6\frac{1}{2}$ in. Amsterdam, Rijksmuseum.

Peter Paul Rubens (1577–1640)
11   Lion Hunt
Panel, $29\frac{1}{8} \times 41\frac{1}{4}$ in. 1615–17. London, National Gallery.

Peter Paul Rubens (1577–1640)
12   The Garden of Love
Pen and ink, washed, touched up with indigo, green and white over black chalk, $19\frac{1}{2} \times 28\frac{1}{2}$ in. respectively. About 1632–34. New York, Metropolitan Museum of Art.

Peter Paul Rubens (1577–1640)
13   "Night" (La Notte): after Michelangelo
Black chalk, pen, heightened with yellow and white bodycolour, $14\frac{1}{8} \times 19\frac{1}{2}$ in. 1603. Paris, Fondation Custodia (F. Lugt Collection).

Peter Paul Rubens (1577–1640)
14   A Fallen Tree
Black chalk and wash, $7\frac{1}{4} \times 12\frac{1}{4}$ in. About 1617–19. Chatsworth, The Duke of Devonshire and the Trustees of the Chatsworth Settlement.

Rembrandt van Rijn (1606–69)
15   (top) A Thatched Cottage
Reed-pen and bistre, in parts rubbed with the finger, $6\frac{7}{8} \times 10\frac{1}{2}$ in. About 1652. Chatsworth, The Duke of Devonshire and the Trustees of the Chatsworth Settlement.

Rembrandt van Rijn (1606–69)
15   (bottom) Farm Buildings beside a Road
Pen in Indian ink, wash, $4\frac{1}{2} \times 7\frac{3}{4}$ in. About 1650. Oxford, Ashmolean Museum.

Anthony Van Dyck (1599–1641)
16   A Study of Cows
Pen and brown ink, with brown wash, $12\frac{1}{2} \times 20\frac{1}{4}$ in. Chatsworth, The Duke of Devonshire and the Trustees of the Chatsworth Settlement.

Jan Brueghel the Elder (1568–1625)
17   View of the Town of Spa
Pen and bistre, washed in bistre, blue, red and Indian ink, $10\frac{1}{8} \times 16\frac{1}{8}$ in. Signed and dated, lower left: Spa Bruegel fec. adi 22 Agosto 1612. Paris, Fondation, Custodia (F. Lugt Collection).

Rembrandt van Rijn (1606–69)
18   The Descent from the Cross
Etching, $20\frac{7}{8} \times 16\frac{1}{8}$ in. 1633.

Rembrandt van Rijn (1606–69)
19   The Death of the Virgin
Etching, $16\frac{1}{8} \times 12\frac{3}{8}$ in. Signed and dated, Rembrandt f. 1639.

Rembrandt van Rijn (1606–69)
20   The Crucifixion ("The Three Crosses")
Etching, $15\frac{1}{8} \times 17\frac{3}{4}$ in. Signed and dated (in third impression only): Rembrandt f. 1653.

Rembrandt van Rijn (1606–69)
21   The Hundred Guilder Print
Etching, $11 \times 15\frac{1}{4}$ in. About 1649.

Peter Paul Rubens (1577–1640)
22   A Gentleman in Armour on Horseback
(Study for the Portrait of the Duke of Lerma)
Pen and ink washed over black chalk, $11\frac{3}{4} \times 8\frac{1}{2}$ in. 1603. Paris, Louvre.

Peter Paul Rubens (1577–1640)
23   A Young Woman with Crossed Hands
Red, black and white chalk, $18\frac{5}{8} \times 14$ in. About 1630. Rotterdam, Boymans-van Beuningen Museum.

Rembrandt van Rijn (1606–69)
24   Sheet of Studies
Pen and wash, red chalk, $3\frac{5}{8} \times 9\frac{1}{8}$ in. About 1636. University of Birmingham, Barber Institute of Fine Arts.

Jacob de Gheyn (1562–1629)
25   Study of Nine Heads
Pen and ink, $14\frac{1}{4} \times 10\frac{1}{4}$ in. Signed and dated 1604, bottom centre. Berlin-Dahlem, Kupferstichkabinett.

Rembrandt van Rijn (1606–69)
26   (top) Saskia's Lying-in Room
Pen and bistre, washes in bistre and Indian ink, heightened with white, $5\frac{5}{8} \times 6\frac{7}{8}$ in. About 1639. Paris, Fondation Custodia (F. Lugt Collection).

Rembrandt van Rijn (1606–69)
26   (bottom) Naked Woman Seated on a Mound
Etching, $7 \times 6\frac{1}{4}$ in. 1631.

Peter Paul Rubens (1577–1640)
27   Study of a Naked Woman, Standing, Seen from the Back
Black and red chalk, with white highlights, $20\frac{1}{8} \times 10$ in. About 1635–40. Paris, Louvre.

Peter Paul Rubens (1577–1640)
28   A Nude Man, Kneeling
Black and white chalk, $20\frac{1}{2} \times 15\frac{3}{8}$ in. About 1609. Rotterdam, Boymans-van Beuningen Museum.

Rembrandt van Rijn (1606–69)
29   (top) Three Studies for a Disciple at Emmaus
Pen and bistre, $6\frac{7}{8} \times 6\frac{1}{4}$ in. About 1633–34. Paris, Foundation Custodia (F. Lugt Collection).

Rembrandt van Rijn (1606–69)
29   (bottom) Head of an Oriental in a Turban, and a Dead Bird of Paradise
Pen and wash in bistre, white bodycolour, $7 \times 6\frac{5}{8}$ in. 1637 (?). Paris, Louvre.

Peter Paul Rubens (1577–1640)
30   Self-Portrait
Black and white chalk, $18\frac{1}{2} \times 11\frac{1}{2}$ in. About 1633–35. Paris, Louvre.

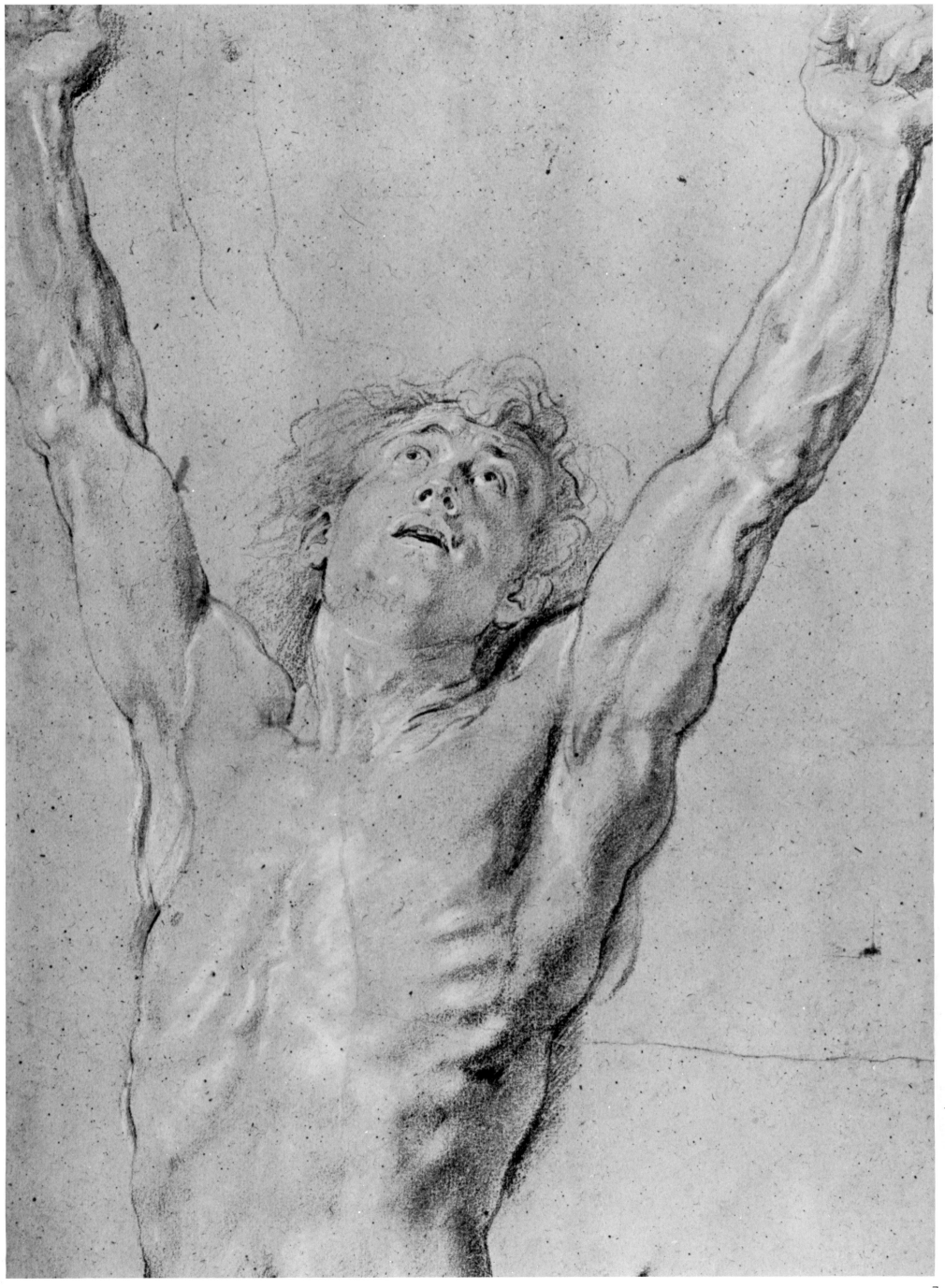

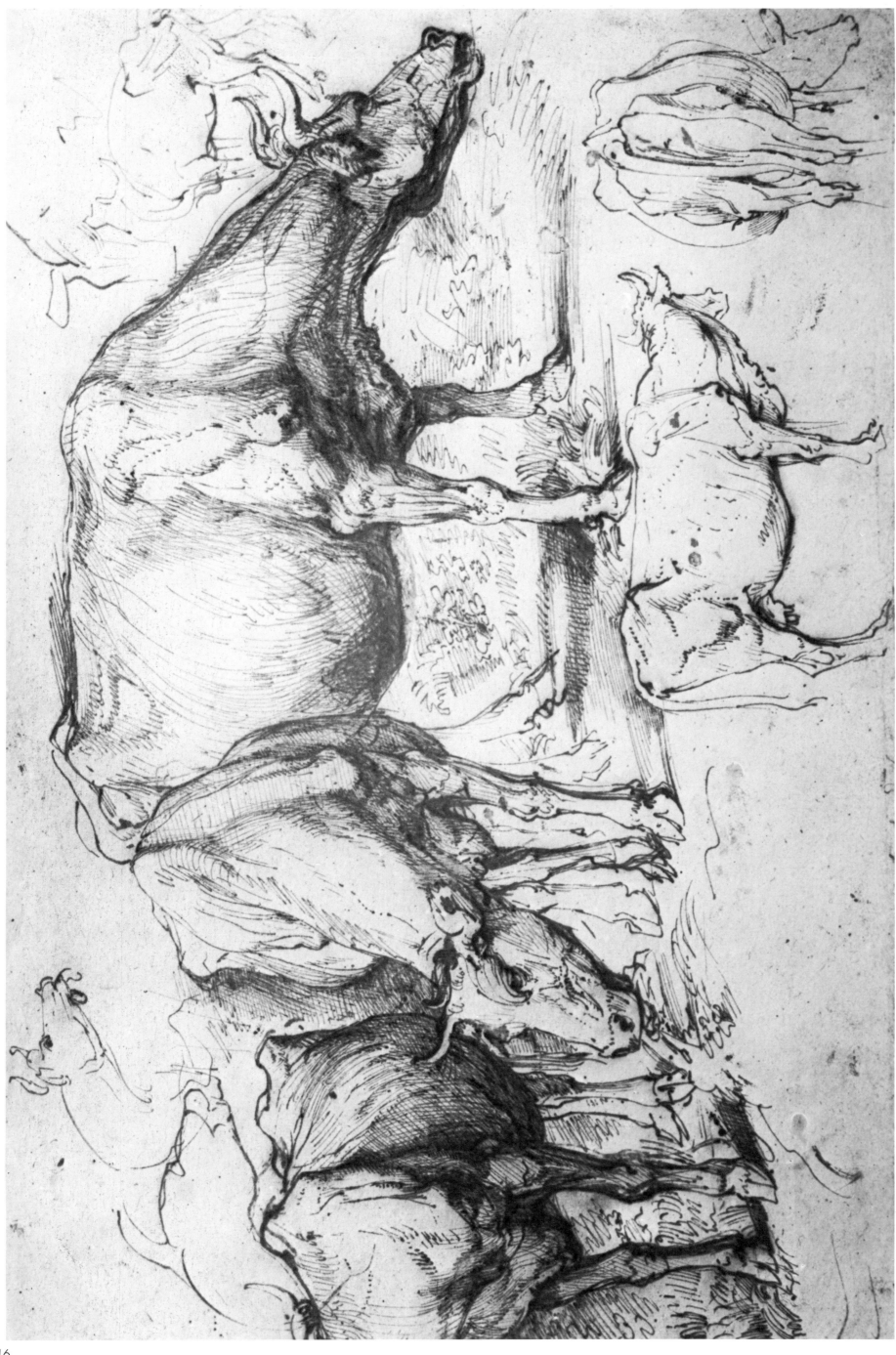

16

23

28

The Colour Plates

The Captions

Ambrosius Bosschaert (1573–1621)
33 A Vase of Flowers
Panel, 25¼ × 18⅛ in. Signed in monogram: AB.
About 1620. The Hague, Mauritshuis.

Jan Brueghel the Elder (1568–1625)
34 A Flemish Fair
Copper, 18¾ × 27 in. Signed and dated 1600.
Royal Collection.

Hendrick Avercamp (1585–1634)
35 A Scene on the Ice near a Town
Panel, 22¾ × 35⅜ in. Signed, on a wooden
boarding in the centre foreground: HA (in monogram). About 1615–20. London, National Gallery.

Peter Paul Rubens (1577–1640)
36 The Rape of the Daughters of Leucippus
Canvas, 87⅝ × 82½ in. About 1618. Munich,
Alte Pinakothek.

Peter Paul Rubens (1577–1640)
37 The Descent from the Cross
Panel, 45 × 30 in. About 1611. London, Courtauld
Institute Galleries.

Peter Paul Rubens (1577–1640)
and Jan Brueghel (1568–1625)
38 Adam and Eve in the Garden of Eden
Panel, 29⅛ × 44⅞ in. Signed: Petri Pauli Rubens . . .
Figr., IBrueghel fec. About 1610–15. The Hague,
Mauritshuis.

Peter Paul Rubens (1577–1640)
39 Crocodile Hunt
Canvas, 97¼ × 126⅜ in. About 1615/16. Munich,
Alte Pinakothek.

Hendrick ter Brugghen (c. 1588–1629)
40 The Concert
Canvas, 39 × 46 in. About 1626–27.
Private Collection.

Rembrandt van Rijn (1606–69)
41 The Risen Christ at Emmaus
Paper on panel, 14⅝ × 16⅛ in. Signed, lower right,
RHL in monogram; about 1628. Paris, Musée Jacque-
mart-André.

Frans Hals (c. 1581/5–1666)
42 Young Man Holding a Skull
Canvas, 36⁵⁄₁₆ × 31¹³⁄₁₆ in. About 1626–28.
Private Collection.

Anthony Van Dyck (1599–1641)
43 Francois Langlois as a Savoyard
Canvas, 41⅛ × 33¼ in. 1632–34(?). The Viscount
Cowdray.

Peter Paul Rubens (1577–1640)
44 Rubens and his Wife, Isabella Brant, in the
Honeysuckle Bower
Canvas, 68½ × 52 in. 1609. Munich, Alte Pinakothek.

Pieter Saenredam (1597–1665)
45 The Interior of the Buurkerk at Utrecht
Panel, 23⅜ × 19¾ in. Signed; de buerckerck binnen
utrecht/aldus geschildert uit iaer 1644/van/Pieter
Saenredam. London, National Gallery.

David Teniers the Younger (1610–90)
46 The Gallery of the Archduke Leopold-Wilhelm
Canvas, 50 × 64 in. Signed, lower left: DAVID
TENIERS Fe/1651. Sussex, Petworth House,
The National Trust.

Gerard ter Borch (1617–81)
47 The Swearing of the Oath of Ratification of the
Treaty of Münster, 15 May 1648
Copper, 17⅞ × 23 in. Signed, on a tablet hanging
on the left hand wall: GTBorch. F. Monasterij. A.
1648. (GTB in monogram). London, National Gallery.

Meindert Hobbema (1638–1709)
48 A Woody Landscape with a Cottage
Canvas, 39⅛ × 51⅜ in. About 1665. London,
National Gallery.

Anthony Van Dyck (1599–1641)
49 Three Heads of Charles I
Canvas 33¼ × 39¼ in. About 1636.
Royal Collection.

Rembrandt van Rijn (1606–69)
50 Self-Portrait
Canvas, 45 × 37 in. About 1669. London, Kenwood
House, Iveagh Bequest.

Peter Paul Rubens (1577–1640)
51 Hélène Fourment in a Fur Wrap (Het Pelsken)
Panel, 69¼ × 32⅝ in. About 1638. Vienna, Kunsthistorisches Museum.

Willem Kalf (1619–93)
52 Still-Life with the Drinking Horn of the
St. Sebastian Archers' Guild, Lobster and Glasses
Canvas, 34 × 40¼ in. About 1653. Private Collection.

Jan Steen (1626–79)
53 Twelfth Night ("Le Roi Boit")
Panel, 23 × 22 in. About 1668. The Marquis of
Tavistock and the Trustees of the Bedford Estates.

Adriaen van Ostade (1610–85)
54 The Interior of a Peasant's Cottage
Panel, 18⅜ × 16⅜ in. Signed, A v Ostade/1668
(Av in monogram). Royal Collection.

Pieter de Hoogh (1629–84)
55 A Woman and her Maid in a Courtyard
Canvas, 29 × 24⅝ in. Signed, lower right: P.D.H./
166(?). London, National Gallery.

Adriaen Brouwer (c. 1606–38)
56 Tavern Scene
Panel, 18⅞ × 29⅞ in. About 1630. London, National
Gallery (on loan from a private collection).

Jan van Goyen (1596–1656)
57 View of Dordrecht
Canvas, 63½ × 100 in. Sussex, Petworth House,
The National Trust.

Aelbert Cuyp (1620–91)
58 River Landscape with Horsemen and Peasants
Canvas, 49 × 96¼ in. Signed, A cuyp. About 1655.
Private Collection.

Johannes Vermeer (1632–75)
59 View of Delft
Canvas, 38⅝ × 40 in. Monogrammed, lower left, on
the boat: IVM. About 1661. The Hague, Mauritshuis.

Johannes Vermeer (1632–75)
60 The Artist in his Studio
Canvas, 51⅛ × 43¾ in. Monogrammed on the map
IVM. About 1665–66. Vienna, Kunsthistorisches
Museum.

Johannes Vermeer (1632–75)
61 Girl Reading a Letter
Canvas, 32⅝ × 25⅜ in. About 1659. Dresden,
Staatliche Gemäldegalerie.

Jacob van Ruisdael (1628/9–82)
62 An Extensive Landscape with a Ruined Castle
and a Village Church
Canvas, 43 × 57½ in. Signed, in the water, lower
right: Jv Ruisdael (JvR in monogram). About 1665–70.
London, National Gallery.

Peter Paul Rubens (1577–1640)
63 Landscape with the Château of Steen
Panel, 51¾ × 90½ in. 1636. London, National
Gallery.

Jacob Jordaens (1593–1678)
64 Portrait of Govaert van Surpele (?) and his
Wife
Canvas, 84 × 74⅜ in. About 1636–37(?). London,
National Gallery.